Heartwarming Accolades

"I rather detest tongue-in-cheek." *Anonymous, Trenton, NJ*

"A true delight! I didn't know half this stuff!" *Eleanor J., Cambridge, MA*

"An appalling intolerance of extortion, adultery, drunk driving, and adult movies. Get a life!" *Ronald K., Las Vegas, NV*

"Without inspiration from this book, I would never have gathered the courage to stand up to my in-laws, Santa Claus, and the Sanitation District. A must read!" *Gerri M., London, UK*

"The most boring book I ever attempted to read!" *Joe B., Birmingham, AL*

"There really are better uses for paper!" *Geroge F., Huntington, WV*

"Wish I could have benefitted from this insight growing up!" *Harry M., Coral Gables, FL*

"If you enjoy this book, you, too, might be a dangerously sick person! What really bothers me is that the writer doesn't even make a token effort to think like a normal person." *Tom R., Topeka, KS*

"Never realized that anyone other than Shakespeare and Aristotle could be a reservoir of so much wisdom." *Emily S., New Haven, CT*

"A must-read for the inquiring mind!" *Jeff C., Des Moines, IA*

"A fairly good book." Jason G., Jasper, WY

"I feel for his poor students!" *Grace N., Atlanta, GA*

"I don't quite agree with everything, but *Delightful Reflections* has made my life at least 14% more meaningful." *Dyvia C., Long Beach, CA.*

"Finally a person under fifty who has the sense to recognize that children should obey their parents!" *Amy Sue R., Jackson, MS*

"Relatively profound." Anne J., Portland, OR

"Better than anything I learned from fortune cookies over the last forty years!" *Anna O., San Francisco, CA*

"I'll never know if there is anything of merit in the second half!" *Thomas D., Boulder, CO*

"Hands down the most bizarre bedtime stories my grandma ever read to me!" *Jennifer K., Honolulu, HI*

"My ex-aunt-in-law told me that this book was a great cure for insomnia. Instead, I ended up laughing all night." *Harry G., Nairobi, Kenya*

Delightful Reflections

Quips, Conjectures, and Pontifications

Lars Perner, Ph.D.

Delightful Reflections: Quips, Conjectures, and Pontifications

ISBN-13: 978-0615561981

by Lars Perner, Ph.D.

First Edition

Copyright 2011 Lars Perner
All rights reserved

Published by Published by Eccenterrific Press
http://www.Eccenterrific.com

Visit Lars Perner's Websites:

http:://www.LarsPerner.com
http:://wwwConsumerPsychologist.com

For more information on purchasing multiple copies of the book for fundraisers and such email Lars Perner at perner@marshall.usc.edu.

Delightful Reflections

Patsy Cline should really confine her walks after midnight to safe areas.

Any residents of Washington, B.C. were most likely Native Americans.

Breaking into a storage facility for prayer books and changing the word "art" within The Lord's Prayer to "ain't" constitutes serious and unconscionable sabotage.

Someone recording a song titled "Girls Don't Want to Have Fun" might be a bit on the dour and puritanical side—or perhaps in denial.

Someone singing "Do Cry for Me, Argentina" is likely rather self-centered.

> Nowadays, Marvin Gaye would have been more likely find out about his significant other's plans to "make [him] blue" through a Facebook status update or a tweet.

> Granting a child's Christmas wish for a hippopotamus would, under most circumstances, be somewhat unkind to his or her parents.

> When a police officer impersonates a neurosurgeon, actually performing an operation should be considered an aggravating factor.

> Morally marginal individuals ought to be aware that what happens in Vegas may stay on Facebook and Youtube for a long time!

A child of a minister who pickets the church with a sign saying that "Prayer is pathetic!" is likely going through a rebellious stage.

Santa Claus has a moral obligation to clean up after his reindeer (or arrange for someone else to do this) so that property owners and city workers are not burdened with this task.

One would hope that a piece of textile with the message that "Dog food is delicious" is a dog coat.

It is mean for parents not to allow their children to clean their rooms.

A product label saying "Made outside China" seems a bit ambiguous.

Few college students today major in rhinoceroserology.

It is doubtful that Alabama Highways would hold quite the same allure.

If you add two even numbers and get an odd result, it is possible that an error was made.

It is morally wrong under most circumstances for criminal defendants to pay aliens from outer space to abduct critical witnesses for the prosecution.

A game called Formville would likely be rather bureaucratic.

A super-soaker water gun fight is not a sufficiently dignified way to settle who is first in the line for the ice cream truck.

Did Rick Springfield ever get over Jesse's girl?

It is morally wrong to send out fake report cards to parents of honor students indicating a straight F average.

It is really sad to hear one elementary school student bragging to another that "My funeral is going to be bigger than your funeral!"

> It is not clear that a sophisticated opera singer would appreciate a compliment of "You rock!"

> Walking up and telling a championship boxer that "Your mother's character needs serious improvement!"—even if true—is an incredibly stupid risk to take.

> One would hope that tensions between a group of picketers outside a Department of Philosophy indignantly carrying signs saying that "Socrates was a psycho!" and counter-demonstrators would not turn into violence.

> For a criminal defendant facing murder charges, an "I ♥ 2 kill" button would most likely more than cancel out the positive impression of wearing a suit and tie.

Profit should be a priority!

A psychiatrist having to break certain news to a patient wearing a button saying "I ♥ being sane!" is not in an enviable position.

Someone who signs a letter to an advice columnist "Measly in Michigan" might have a self esteem problem.

Authors who are afraid of the dark should refrain from hiring ghostwriters.

It is highly unethical to falsely claim that seven medical studies all show that a new brand of cigarettes is an effective cure for lung cancer— especially if the research actually shows that this brand is more dangerous than other brands.

> Hopefully, Rikki didn't lose that number!

> A question found in an online file might be considered a downloaded question.

> One rarely ever hears any objection being expressed to the comparison of pears and grapefruits.

> It is usually not a good idea to tell one's spouse that "I kinda love you!"

> It seems rather arrogant to reflexively tell a neighbor that "My granddaughter's character is morally superior to that of your granddaughter" without knowing anything about one's neighbor's granddaughter.

It would have been ironic if Lynn Anderson had actually promised a tulip garden.

To minimize the risk of injury, it might be helpful to move one's tongue before turning the other cheek.

It is saddening to hear about the end of Neil's relationship with Melinda. Hopefully, Shilo has by now been able to help him find "a girl who'll stay and won't play games behind [him]."

Grandmothers who rob drug dealers at gunpoint to finance their knitting clubs should realize that two wrongs do not make a right! They really have an obligation to turn over the evidence they have gathered to the police rather than taking the law into their own hands.

An individual wearing a T-shirt which, on the front, says "I ♥ driving on the wrong side of the road!" and on the back says "I can't stand kangaroos!" would be well advised to head to the UK, Hong Kong, Japan, Barbados, or Singapore rather than Australia.

To "inaccess" does not yet appear to have become an accepted verb in the English language.

One rarely ever hears of anyone going muleback riding.

It seems more appropriate for a Dachshund than for a Golden Retriever to wear a dog coat inscribed "I ♥ being a Dachshund!"

Sucker moms are vulnerable to manipulation.

The idea of a Modern Dinosaur Association does not seem very impressive.

My nephews appear to be too modest to brag that "My uncle is cooler than your uncle!"

It seems rather unkind and confrontational to ask a minister, "Do you seriously believe that?"

It would likely be rather demoralizing to arrive without reservation at restaurant with a long line of people waiting to be seated, being told immediately that "Your table is ready," and then being led to a table with a big sign saying "Reserved For Rednecks."

It really wouldn't "be nice if we were older."

If Lynn Anderson suddenly has a memory of this, the decent thing to do is to record "I DID Promise You a Rose Garden."

It really should not be necessary for a writer to add the lyrics that "Just because you don't think this song's about you doesn't [sic] mean that you're not vain!"

If it does not look like a Dachshund, does not walk like a Dachshund, and does not bark like a Dachshund, it might be considered deceptive to list it on Craigslist as a Dachshund without disclosing these material facts.

When taunted by an acquaintance that "My grandmother can beat up your grandmother," it is inconsiderate to ask one's grandmother to prove that the opposite is true—quite possibly to both the grandmothers in question.

There does not seem to be a compelling reason to call Ghost Busters when there's nothing strange in the neighborhood.

It is incredibly stupid for petty criminals to bring attention to themselves by wearing T-shirts saying "Doughnuts are disgusting!"

It is highly unethical for a hospital to "plant" a medical looking individual in a lab coat reading Dialysis for Dummies in the patient/visitor cafeteria of a competing hospital.

It would have been even more sad if Terry Jacks had sung "We didn't have joy, we didn't have fun, we didn't have seasons in the sun."

If the Personnel Director of a firm buys a used car, for her own safety and to reduce the threat of wrongful termination lawsuits, she should remove any bumper stickers saying things like "I ♥ terminating people!" and "Firing employees is fun!"

A nun who wakes up the whole neighborhood while beating up a fellow nun for disturbing the peace needs a serious talk by the mother superior about goal displacement and constructive ways to deal with problem co-workers.

It seems perfectly reasonable for a Dachshund to growl in disapproval at a group of picketers carrying big signs saying "Being a Dachshund is way uncool!"

Delightful Reflections

An individual who goes walking before midnight is less likely to run into Patsy Cline.

Most people could not truthfully wear a button saying "I ♥ liver!"

Traitor Joe's might carry things like Cuban cigars, North Korean Ginseng, Libyan figs, and Iranian dates.

Even if it walks like a duck, quacks like a duck, and looks like a duck, one should try to make a greater profit on it than one would ordinarily make on a duck.

It is not a good idea to challenge a police officer to a doughnut eating contest.

The vast majority of students who complain about grades probably don't realize how little their work would impress Shania Twain.

It is difficult to understand the rationale for boxing. If you want to be civilized, why not agree not to fight in the first place? If you don't want to be civilized, why have rules?

There ought to be something like Prudebook.com that would automatically replace all profanity in postings with the phrase "[expletive deleted]."

A "Table of Discontents" in a book would seem to be a strong indication that the publisher lacks confidence that it will be well received.

"You're 1.9% sweeter than average!" might not be a particularly effective endearment.

For people who find bear hunting boring, it seems rather deceptive to wear a T-shirt saying "I ♥ bear hunting!" just to be fashionable.

There does not appear to be any support in respected, peer reviewed journals for the hypothesis that a pear a day keeps the dentist away.

Cain may have been the first communist.

A geeky lifeguard might save more files than lives.

Saying that cynics are dime a dozen seems rather cynical.

A fifth grade student who excitedly calls her parents from the principal's office on a cold winter day to announce with pride that "I hosed down seven classmates and the school librarian for using profanity today!" really needs a good talk on constructive, non-confrontational, and non-violent approaches to achieving worthy objectives.

A tweet by someone with a large number of followers that "My [expletive deleted] ex-aunt-in-law is a [expletive deleted] sinner!" may seriously impede healing in both extended families.

People who live to kill should get a life.

A sanity disadvantaged Beatles fan might hum "I Am the Walnut" in the shower.

It would probably be a mistake for the TSA to make an exception and let a passenger bring a gun aboard a flight just because she wears a button saying "I ♥ being a saint!"

A button saying "It's OK not to wear purple!" would seem to have rather limited information value.

If the sun is shining, it would seem to logically follow that she ain't gone.

When in Rome, one should try to make a profit on the Romans.

Conceiving of a logically compelling rationale for the hypothesis that a mango a day (for the owner) keeps the veterinarian away seems rather difficult.

A concert at which hip hop singer Chel C opened for country singers Hill and Billy Clinton would likely be rather eclectic.

Psycho-tourism—including activities such as blowing up historical sites, hunting endangered species, counterfeiting the local currency, teaching children profanity, littering, disturbing the peace, armed robbery, stealing hotel towels, and spitting on senior citizens—is morally unjustifiable.

New Yorkers would probably not look kindly on an "I Used 2 ♥ NY" button.

It would have been nice if Carly could have clarified whether, if attending a party on a yacht, one should walk aboard as if walking into a party or as if walking onto a yacht.

Most likely, members of the Association of Atheist Adulterers of Alabama would not bother to read the Bibles in their hotel rooms during illicit visits.

An "I Used 2B Sane" button would probably be an effective tool for an elementary school teacher looking for an extended paid leave pending a thorough psychiatric examination.

A band recording "Do Stop Believing" may either consist of cynics or rebels against Journey.

> In practice, most Protestant congregations probably spend much more time singing hymns than picketing.

> Do actions actually speak louder than words spoken on a PA system?

> It would be highly unethical and deceptive for Pandora.com to send packages with fake return addresses in order to trick unsuspecting recipients into opening them.

> If it walks like a duck, looks like a Dachshund, and quacks like a duck, it is difficult to tell what it is.

> A duck in a philosophical mood might reflect "Quackigo ergo sum."

It is difficult to tell if a button saying "It's OK not to care!" is an indication of tolerance, apathy, or both.

If it looks like the Aflac Duck, walks like the Aflac Duck, and quacks "Aflac!" like the Aflac Duck, it probably is the Aflac Duck.

It is advisable—if it doesn't look like a duck, walk like a duck, and quack like a duck—to hold off on definitively declaring it a duck until genetic testing confirms that it is a duck.

Picketers at the Beethoven Festival carrying big banners saying that "Beethoven was a bozo!" are likely trying to be contrarians.

> If it looks like a turkey, walks like a turkey, and gobbles like a turkey, it is probably not a duck.

> On Halloween, if it walks like a duck and quacks like a duck but looks too big to be a duck, it is probably a trick-or-treater.

> If it looks like a zebra and doesn't quack like a duck, one will probably not need to see how it walks to conclude that it is a zebra.

> If it kinda looks like a duck, kinda walks like a duck, and kinda quacks like a duck, one might not be as confident that it actually is a duck.

> One might be confused if it quacks but not like a duck.

If it looks like a rubber duck, it probably does not walk and will probably only quack if it is the deluxe model.

It would be mean for a geek to taunt old farmer McDonald with the words that "My virtual duck can quack louder than your old fashioned one!"

If it looks like a duck and walks like a duck but does not seem to quack, it may still be a duck.

It is doubtful that quacking is productive under most circumstances if you are not a duck.

A duck might resent people engaging in speciel profiling in presuming that it quacks.

> It is entirely plausible that all ducks are created equal, no matter how they look, walk, and quack.

> If it looks like duck pond and one frequently hears quacks, it probably is a duck pond.

> A bumper sticker saying "You can change the world, but why bother?" seems rather cynical.

> If it looks like a goose, walks like a goose, and quacks, it may be imitating a duck.

> If it looks like a parrot, flies like a parrot, and quacks like a duck, it is more likely to be a parrot.

It is quite reasonable for ministers to "bench" members of the choir who show up for services in a state of intoxication.

It is very inappropriate for airline pilots to compete who can drink the most during a transcontinental flight—especially if restroom trips are permitted underway.

Realistically, most professors should probably stay in the educational environment rather than trying to "find a rock 'n' roll band that needs a helping hand."

It would be very bad news for the government—and might raise some due process questions—if the Supreme Court posted a sign at its entrance saying "No Solicitors General."

Rednail women are more likely to wear sunscreen than redneck ones.

It must be demoralizing to be a mediocrehero.

Is a substandard deviation decisively bad or just a very small variation?

Is there a parallel universe that features pink tea and green lemonade?

Someone who testifies at her sentencing hearing that "Mugging Sunday school teachers is cool" likely has significant problems with authority, a rather poor character, a seriously messed up value system, little if any genuine feeling of remorse, and self-preservation skills that are, at best, impoverished.

Residents of Albany might resent having their city referred to as "The Puny Apple."

A T-shirt saying "My Parents Are Pathetic!" is likely a violation of the Fifth Commandment.

A painting titled "Definitely a Dachshund" might very likely feature a Dachshund.

If Joan Jett no longer loves rock 'n' roll, she might consider recording "I Loved Rock 'n' Roll."

It seems inconsiderate to set up a computer store in someone's home without first getting his or her consent.

A TV series titled The Real Housewives of Des Moines might be a bit on the corny side.

If Van Morrison had been less enthusiastic, he might have sung that "It's a fairly decent night for a moondance."

Under some circumstances, it may be perfectly appropriate for a veterinarian to order a CAT scan for a dog.

If only more students would believe in the doctrine of professorial infallibility!

Benefits of becoming a Registered Redneck are likely rather limited.

Having a black tie event at the Rowdy Redneck Restaurant might be a form of reverse snobbery.

It really seems entirely reasonable to lock the door if Paul McCartney stays out until 2:45 a.m.

One might be somewhat uncomfortable with a surgeon using an obsolete operating system such as MS-DOS or CP/M.

Most rednecks do not rock. More likely, they are into country.

Many junior high school girls would probably be willing to pay extortion money to their aunts and uncles in return for not being picked up from school in a car with a bumper sticker saying "My niece is the lead singer of Dorky Destiny."

A claim by a defense attorney representing thugs being prosecuted for assault that "Concussions are good for the soul" is entirely without merit.

If someone signing the name "Nutcase in Newark" had written Ann Landers bemoaning the "irrationally excessive emphasis that society places on sanity," she would probably have recommended counseling.

It would really be more considerate of the saints to walk in softly rather than marching—especially if they arrive early in the morning.

It is hard to imagine that anyone but a highly arrogant traditionalist would want to sing a song called "What a Declining World" with lyrics including "They'll know so much less than I already know."

If Noah had been a mathematician, we would probably have heard about his arcsine.

Pep Boys would probably be perceived as more politically correct if renamed Pep Children.

Despite a reputation for attention to detail, Japanese chefs often forget to cook the fish.

A significant difference between a baby and a handgun is that the baby does not come with a silencer.

Elton is excellent.

The Puny Panda Restaurant would probably serve rather small meals.

It is ordinarily not a good idea to do business with individuals who have more than three RICO felony convictions.

It really does not seem all that insulting to tell a pink farm animal that "You're a pig!"

In truth, most people would probably prefer, if possible, not to encounter an alligator in the future.

There is nothing wrong with remaining an odd person. Getting even is much over-rated!

For people whose only joy in life is cutting people up, it is a more responsible choice to become a surgeon than a serial killer.

A summer-wonderland is much preferable to a winter one.

Happiness is giving a mother of all midterms.

Picketing in-laws' homes over minor issues is usually a bad idea.

A beautiful exam can be almost as beautiful as a beautiful woman.

A divorced man who gives his children T-shirts saying that "My mom is meaner than your mom" would appear to be engaging in highly dysfunctional passive aggression.

Criminal defendants should refrain from telling the judge to "Shut your [expletive deleted] mouth."

Residents of one bedroom apartments who are thinking about renting a rhinoceros should seriously reconsider.

The Real Housewives really ought to treat each other with greater kindness and compassion.

Craig might never have had a list if he had been less organized.

Marrying an individual whose conviction for the homicide of a former spouse was overturned because the police failed to properly read the Miranda Warning is likely to be a bad idea.

A candidate running on the platform that "Peace is pathetic" should probably not be elected.

It is better to take Vitamin A than Vitamin F before an exam.

Serial killing should be discouraged under most circumstances.

Domain name brokers are virtual estate agents.

If it quacks like a duck, telling it to be quiet probably won't be effective.

It would be rather sad if Billy Ocean has reverted to the belief that love is just a fairytale.

> Normal people rarely ever make history.

> I recommend empathy for eccentrics.

> The White House is a much nicer destination than the big house.

> Aside from the ethical problems that this practice entails, serial killing is a waste of time.

> The elimination of competitors by shark feeding or firing squad is illegal in most states.

> If elected President of the United States, Paul Simon should probably reconsider his plan to put a notice on the Presidential podium that "[his] mother loves [him]."

One should hesitate to patronize an establishment offering misfortune cookies.

Outsourcing the protection of the President to Victoria's Secret Service is not advisable.

A dysfunctional MRI is unlikely to be reliable.

I am too far away from the school yard to be able to see Paul and Julio.

It is rather doubtful that an application for a study titled "Consumers Who Kill: Participant Observation of the Lifestyles of Serial Murderers" would receive Institutional Review Board (IRB) approval.

> One rarely ever sees a vending machine with a sign saying "In Order."

> Adulterers should be retroactively denied Halloween candy and be required to pay back what they have received with interest.

> It is unfair to charge parsimonious bank customers an underdraft fee.

> The reprehensible demotion of Pluto from its rightful status as a planet is a thinly veiled slight at eccentrics. It makes little sense that a pathetic planet like Mercury—which has no moons—gets to be a planet when Pluto—which has four moons—does not. Will school children now resort to the mnemonic "My very excellent mother just served us NOTHING?"

A minister who suffers from laryngitis is in poor condition to preach to the choir.

Many people probably prefer to have their calls, rather than letters, returned.

It is doubtful that more than 15% of American homes are actually haunted by ghosts.

An online site called Faithbook might make those without faith feel excluded.

Hot curry might be described as non-mellow yellow.

The Fundamental Human Need is for chocolate.

Adulterers who park in front of fire hydrants while on illicit errands deserve to be towed.

Professors would really have appreciated it if the Ten Commandments would have included a prohibition against surfing the Internet during class.

Someone who wears a T-shirt saying "Hit Internet objects—not people!" is more likely to be a geek than a sissy.

Being normal is not a badge of distinction.

Adulterers are sinful psychos.

A wife or girlfriend will probably not appreciate being told that "You look relatively beautiful today."

In most civilian occupations, carrying more than two guns to work tends to be overkill.

There does not seem to be a compelling reason for people who are not hungry to have breakfast at Tiffany's.

A tax on chocolate would likely amount to an unconstitutional deprivation of substantive due process.

Cursing is contemptible.

Profanity is pathetic.

Using a counterfeit ticket to ride is morally wrong.

Adulterers should be ineligible for opera season tickets.

People should repent their sins rather than bragging about them on Facebook.

An ensemble going door to door singing "I'm dreaming of a pink Christmas" might very well be sponsored by Avon, Revlon, or a sorority.

It would be helpful for some people if attention were put on sale.

Delightful Reflections

> *Expletives should be deleted.*

> It would be ethically problematic to offer the people next door who are trying to sell their home to take down one's "NastyNeighbor.com" banner in return for $25,000.

> Good Americans would have to strongly disapprove of an un-American Express card that made a donation of one percent of all charges to the Communist Party.

> On the average, philanthropists tend to have somewhat better characters than philanderers.

> Antarctica is too good for adulterers, serial extortionists, burglars, bad children, and students who gossip during class.

Psychopaths who sell military secrets to the enemy are traitor trash.

There would be serious ethical objections to a university that bought a list of SAT takers and then charged a non-application fee to those who did not apply there.

It really wasn't kind of Rod to tell Maggie that "The sun in [her] eyes really [showed] [her] age."

One should be skeptical of testimony for the prosecution by an individual who lives next to the defendant and wears a button saying "I ♥ bearing false witness against my neighbor!"

Dumping manure on the driveways of accounting professors—no matter how boring their classes—is inconsiderate and morally wrong.

Serving human dinner guests canned dog food would ordinarily be considered a violation of social norms.

Attorneys who show up to court intoxicated deserve to be disbarred.

Puffin' is pathetic!

If someone claims to be a police officer but cannot produce a receipt for doughnuts, one might reasonably doubt the authenticity of the badge that he or she presents.

Voters in certain states really should be more conscientious about putting sunscreen on their necks.

The owner of a blog named Adorable Princess likely has considerable ego.

For youthful individuals, a youth hostel is probably preferable to an establishment that is youth hostile.

Having a pathetic profile is likely to be a source of some disappointment.

A document requesting classified information ostensibly signed by Admiral A. Archibald Andrews, United States Air Force, is probably a forgery.

Disturbing the peace is disruptive.

Selling Patriot Missiles to the government of North Korea is unpatriotic.

A TV series titled The Average Wife would most likely not be particularly successful.

Proof found outside the pudding is likely to be much less messy.

A web site at GrandmasLittlePsycho.com would likely feature rather unwholesome content.

Students who gossip during class are disgusting, morally repugnant psychopaths.

> The Tiny Wall of Taiwan may not be all that impressive.

> Halloween is probably an unpleasant day for healthnut parents.

> Most parents would probably be resentful of a book titled The Joy of Junk Food.

> It is a rather ominous sign if a child says that "Fraud is fun."

> It is quite unseemly for grandparents and grandchildren to engage in armed robbery together (even if that is the only interest they have in common).

Bad is not beautiful!

Children who brag about obstructing justice deserve punishment rather than praise.

Is there some parallel universe in which major cartoon figures are Patrick Pig and Ducky Duck?

Some element of goal displacement is likely involved in a bumper sticker proclaiming that "My pastor can beat up your pastor!"

It is doubtful that anyone lives in the orange submarine.

Spending more than three hours a week speaking with aliens from space is likely to be rather unproductive.

One should probably look with suspicion on a book with the title All I Ever Really Needed to Know I Learned on Reality TV.

It would be rather disconcerting to be screened at the airport by officials wearing "Transportation Insecurity Administration" badges.

Most people are not entirely certain of the implications of Heisenberg's Uncertainty Principle.

In July in Orlando it is actually rather awful weather for a sleigh ride together with you.

> Being sent to a Catholic military boarding school in North Dakota is likely to send bad children a powerful message.

> First time undercover police officers will likely experience serious doughnut withdrawal.

> Under the majority of circumstances, dueling is a relatively unconstructive method of resolving minor disputes.

> "I can't help killing" should be considered at best a marginal excuse.

> One rarely ever sees any Salvation Air Force or Salvation Navy facilities. Are these too classified to be identified as such?

If a disproportionate number of bad people are struck by lightning, that would be evidence of the Theory of the Survival of the Morally Fittest.

It seems unnecessarily provocative, perhaps except under the most unusual circumstances, to have one's children wear a T-shirt saying "All I Want for Christmas is a Better Grandma" during visits to in-laws that occur before October.

Debbie's dad's disgustingly disobedient deluxe Dachshund doesn't deserve delicious doggie dishes.

In practice, a Requesting Officer might not be all that effective.

A band called Too Awful is likely either very modest or extremely bad.

The Magic Republic would be a name more consistent with American values of democracy.

An organization calling itself Recycling Rednecks would likely collect a lot of beer cans and bottles.

Running false obituaries of people who never existed in the first place is, at best, questionably ethical.

Will the undercover authorities, when they are ready to give Michael Westin his old job back, issue a chill notice?

An organization called Paleontologists Without Partners would seem rather parochial.

Profit is good for the soul.

Can we truly be dust in the wind on days when the wind is not blowing?

It is difficult to tell if someone who says that "My grandmother-in-law is more obnoxious than your grandmother-in-law" is bragging or expressing exasperation.

Some people might find it fun to picket with big signs saying that "Life is boring!"

It is probably not sufficient to tell a spouse or family member who is receiving a major award that "I am relatively impressed for the time being."

It would likely be difficult to get people to root for a sports team named the Boston Bozos.

Attorneys might like a search engine named Suegle.com to help them find plaintiffs and defendants.

It is doubtful that someone who feels the need to insist that "I'm saner than you are!" is.

Someone who says that "If I don't have fun killing people I dislike, someone else will" can reasonably be deemed a cynical psycho.

It is relatively unethical for process servers to dress up as Santa Claus.

> A large A should be superimposed to Arnold's painting in the gallery of former California Governors!

> It is inappropriate for graduates to text with one hand while they are receiving their diploma with the other.

> The "Porky Pig Song" is probably not performed all that frequently in Anaheim and Orlando.

> It may not be appropriate for a church to sell popcorn to people entering the service.

> It would likely be considered a violation of social norms—at least by some people—to sell tickets to a funeral.

It is irresponsible to give materials to make explosives to rebellious grandparents just so that they will stop pestering one.

A silent auction is really preferable to a loud and obnoxious one.

It is helpful to remind children that they will be less likely to receive coal in their stockings if they spend the summer studying in preparation for next year's classes.

An organization called Fencing Contractors Without Borders would seem rather ironic.

If Donald Trump might be interested diversifying by getting into waste disposal, he could open Donald's Dump.

Is Statewide on your side, too?

One really doesn't need to feel much sympathy for people who bemoan that "There's such a social stigma to being a murderer for hire!"

Certain insecure people likely post status symbol updates.

A "Get Into Jail Free" card would probably not command particularly high bids on eBay.

Someone who wears a T-shirt saying "My Dachshund can't stand your Dachshund!" is quite possibly the owner of a grumpy and non-social Dachshund.

Chopsticks—despite the best of intentions—were a really stupid invention!

It would be a rather bad sign for the petitioner if the judge starts out the announcement of his or her decision with the words "Petitioner is pathetic."

The City of New Orleans should be ashamed of the House of the Rising Sun and should take measures to get this place of evil shut down!

The chef at a restaurant whose menu lists "Eels of Eden" would probably not be known for his or her modesty.

I ♥ $, ¥, €, & £.

Seeing a membership placard from the Badder Business Bureau in a store is not particularly comforting.

An attorney hoping for a unanimous decision in his or her favor should not arrive for oral argument at the Supreme Court in a vehicle with a bumper sticker saying "Ruth is a redneck!"

One should generally not trust the President of Mercenaries for Peace.

Grandmothers who take "My grandma is a super-pscyho" as a compliment are quite reprehensible.

It is most likely not productive to speculate on how long one would last on Broadway.

Assault with a non-deadly weapon is still a morally reprehensible offense!

One should be careful not to annoy members of the Association of Vengeful Vegetarians picketing with a sign saying that "Just because we don't kill animals doesn't mean we don't kill people!"

If someone can truthfully say that "My grandma arrested your grandma for disturbing the peace and hauled her off to jail," his or her grandmother is likely employed in law enforcement, volunteers in law enforcement, or performed a citizen's arrest.

It is possible—albeit unlikely—that Ronnie Redneck and Billy Bob Bozo are opera, rather than country, singers.

Even if smoking a dynamite stick is highly fashionable, it is a very stupid practice which is also incredibly inconsiderate of innocent bystanders.

One rarely ever sees a sign at a restaurant saying "Voted Worst Burger....!"

If someone brings a big elephant to class, there will be a big elephant in the classroom.

It would be rather ironic if the Alabama Atheist Association held a joint fundraiser with the Colorado Christian Club.

One rarely ever hears about the Permitted City.

It would be prudent to doubt the authenticity of a check ostensibly drawn on the Bank of Antarctica.

The author of The Joy of Jail would likely be either an extreme positive thinker or offer very unwholesome advice.

When a neurosurgeon impersonates a police officer, actually performing arrests should be considered an aggravating factor.

Under all but the most unusual circumstances, it is inconsiderate of students to bring gorillas to class.

A song titled "Eleanor Pigby" might be about someone who likes to wear pink and/or litter.

> It is prudent to prepare children for the possibility that Santa Claus may get with it and start outsourcing deliveries in the near future.

> It would be extremely unethical to aid the conspiracy of physicians to buy up the entire world harvest of apples.

> A song titled "Fairly Good Vibrations" seems a bit lacking in enthusiasm.

> Members of Nutcases Against Sanity might well be seriously messed up bozos with a major attitude problem.

> A Bloodless Mary would likely lack tomato juice.

The owner of a car with a bumper sticker saying "I ♥ debits and credits!" or "I ♥ depreciating people's assets!" is probably an accountant.

It is rather ironic that U2 is sometimes found listed first in the U section.

Someone who has devoted his or her career to the study of gossip might be called a gossippologist.

It is a sign of an incredibly seriously messed up belief system to wear a T-shirt saying that "Believing professors is stupid!"

It would be rather disillusioning if it turns out the e actually only equals approximately mc squared.

Life was clearly much less satisfying before the advent of USB ports.

It would seem rather demoralizing to live in Garbageville in Dumpster County.

There may not be such a thing as a subatomic clock.

It would be at least somewhat unethical to sell non-season tickets that would actually not be valid for any event.

Children who represent their behavior at home as "civil disobedience" should still be punished.

A law requiring apartment complexes to offer free forklift parking for their tenants is, on the balance, a bad idea.

Someone named Tiffany would likely have breakfast at Tiffany's often.

Being a donkey-whisperer is probably somewhat less prestigious.

Under most circumstances, it would be inappropriate for police officers to squirt water guns at citizens not suspected of criminal activity.

A clothing line called Dorky Destiny would probably not be popular with teenagers and pre-teens.

Donating one's soul is probably morally unacceptable, too (especially if motivated by a tax deduction).

Canceling a trip to the dentist might not be an appropriate—let alone effective—way to discipline a misbehaving child.

A statement that a nutritional supplement is "97% poison free" does not seem all that reassuring.

The historical record does not appear to hold evidence of the existence of the Wizard of Osaka.

Most people know considerably less about the aesthetics of Spain than Daniel does.

There really isn't a good reason to represent a concoction of vinegar and water as lemonade if one is offered free lemons.

It is rather presumptuous to ask one's friends with diplomatic immunity to whack disliked others.

It is usually not advisable to wear a gorilla suit to a job interview.

The title of Discount of Monte Cristo would not be all that prestigious.

Giving a personals profile the title of "Boring bozo" might be an honest, but not particularly effective, approach for boring bozos.

One can go for months without seeing a bumper sticker saying that "My child is a shame student at ___ School."

Courses on second aid seem to be offered rarely if at all.

Drug dealers and other rotten psychopaths would likely prefer the slogan "Just say yes!"

Although there is some value to multi-tasking, texting while exchanging wedding wows is not recommended.

It is both immodest and pathetic to brag that "My life is 13.5% more meaningful than your life!"

It is not at all unreasonable to question the fairness of a first come-last served policy.

It would not in children's interest to send traceable text messages telling their school principals to "Grow up!"

Picketers carrying signs saying "Protest Peace!" are likely misguided.

Being issued a Non-Learning Permit by the Department of Motor Vehicles might be considered a not so subtle indication of lack of confidence.

A Parliament Committee on un-Australian Activities would just not have quite the same ring to it.

The argument that to make high speed car chases fair, the police should give the offender a ten minute break every two hours to refuel and go to the restroom does not seem all that persuasive.

It would likely be very frustrating to traitors to hack into a wifi spot named "Strategic NSA Black Op" only to discover that there was nothing—not even an Internet connection—on the other side.

Decent society ought to disapprove of the memberships of both Serial Killers Against Communism and Communists Against Serial Killing.

A Deluxe Dachshund may not be much better than a regular one.

Confessing to the murder of people who are not dead would likely be considered obstruction of justice rather than a good deed.

Without the proper telescope filters, it is really not safe to check if there's a little black spot on the Sun today.

Few people seem to talk about having an average hair day.

It hardly seems appropriate to wait for a preventive health specialist whose next available appointment is in fourteen years.

It is not clear that WD53 is better than WD50, let alone WD52.

It takes a special someone to appreciate the romanticism of a stapler or box of file folders as a Valentine's gift.

It is highly inconsiderate to dump skeletons from one's closet into someone else's trash receptacle that will clearly run out of space before the next collection day.

There are probably people who have been there but haven't done that.

Under most circumstances, it is morally wrong to hose down senior citizens on their way to church, synagogue, or mosque.

The campaign slogan "Preempt Peace!" seems rather cynical.

It would be mean to go breaking Elton John's heart when he has specifically asked one not to do this.

A tour operator offering "Boring Beijing" trips would likely appeal to a relatively small segment.

Why do some people insist that Christmas decorations should not go up until after July 4? Do they have an aversion to being jolly?

The owner of a car with a bumper sticker saying "My heroes have always been reference librarians!" probably either (1) is a reference librarian, (2) is married to one, (3) has a son or daughter of that profession, (4) is rather geeky, (5) is otherwise eccentric, and/or (6) bought the car used.

An impartial derivative would seem more credible.

It is generally not a good idea to use unconditioner after shampooing.

It does not seem all that impressive to be listed in the Antisocial Register.

One ought to be rather skeptical of a claim that the U.S. Census is unconstitutional.

A drunken police officer who pulls over a motorist for reckless driving could be said to be acting hypocritically.

A huge billboard admonishing people to "REPENT 14% OF YOUR SINS!" seems to be a bit on the lenient side.

It ought to constitute severely aggravating circumstances for a serial killer to repeatedly ignore with impunity environmental impact assessment requirements of lead bullets.

Nasty people might like to see an Incivil Rights Act.

One should not necessarily be overly impressed by someone saying "My grandmother killed more people last week than your grandmother!" It could be that she shot a single burglar and has killed fewer than a half dozen people during the past sixty years of her life.

Former revolutionaries who now call out to "Profit on the People!" appear to have undergone a change in fundamental values.

A book with the title Chicken Soup for the Vegetarian Soul might not make a lot of sense.

Is Greek yogurt popular at fraternities and sororities?

Should the study of automobile wrecking yards be considered junk science?

The proposition that "For every ethical argument, there is an opposite but not necessarily equal counter-argument" might entail some singularity problems.

Extortion by larceny, assault with or without a deadly weapon, and conspiracy to restrain trade are grossly inconsiderate acts.

A meeting scheduled to start at "6:00 a.m. dull" probably will not start on time.

Obstruction of justice is very inconsiderate.

Children who file suit against Santa Claus would appear both incredibly ungrateful and severely deficient in holiday spirit.

Someone who sought an injunction prohibiting Santa Claus from coming to town would likely be unpopular.

It is unnecessarily mean and spiteful to tell Mary that her little lamb is "incredibly puny" and will "make pathetic lamb chops."

The credibility as a moral philosopher of someone who says that "The means justify the ends" seems questionable.

There is little comfort in the word "relatively" when given the heads-up that "A relatively serious psycho stopped by to see you."

Applicants for the Peace Corps would be well advised not bring a copy of Guns & Ammo to read in the interview waiting room.

A merchant offering a "Buy One, Get Fourteen Free" deal is probably rather eager to reduce inventory (or grossly over-priced to begin with).

There really doesn't seem to be much of a point in joining Whackos Without Vision.

Delightful Reflections

> It is extremely irresponsible to sell dynamite sticks to children under age eleven—especially if they do not have a note from their parents allowing them to buy these.

> Wearing a sweatshirt saying "World's Worst Grandma" would likely be motivated by poor self esteem, a distorted value system, or a bizarre sense of humor.

> People who consider cannibalism cool have a seriously messed up value system. If that is a judgmental, ethnocentric, and narrow-minded viewpoint, so be it!

> It is unfair to give a sweatshirt saying "World's Worst Grandmother" to someone who is actually only the 119th worst grandmother in the world.

An individual who resolves to make 14% fewer arbitrary decisions during the coming year may be off to a rather unpromising start.

Children would greatly benefit from discovering just how much more meaningful their lives will be if they obey their parents!

An umbrella vendor in a business district which is largely deserted on week-ends might sing that "Sunny days and Fridays always get me down!"

Politically correct lyrics can become a bit cumbersome—consider, for example: "In the meadow we can build a snowperson/We'll pretend that he or she is Parson or Parsonelle Brown/He or she'll say: Are you married?/We'll say: No, person/...."

Delightful Reflections

There would be a significant change in meaning if a slight lyrics change were made to "You puny town of Bethlehem."

Math teachers would be justified in taking offense to a bumper sticker saying "Reciprocals are for rednecks!"

The world would probably not have turned out all that differently if Neil Diamond had recorded "October Aftern."

Oliver Tiwst is setting a bad example for today's children with his greed and lack of gratitude.

In some parallel universe, "Rudolph, the Redhorned Rhino" may be a popular Christmas song.

It is rather sad to hear an elementary school student taunting a classmate that "My grandma will be eligible for parole before your grandma!"

Sadly, parties to a nasty divorce might sing that "It's lovely weather for a sleigh ride without you."

Students tend not to be greatly comforted by reassurance that "You will definitely not receive a grade below F."

A Christmas Carol would be greatly improved by the addition of the Ghost of Christmas Profit.

Riding a hippopotamus in the Macy's Christmas Parade is not safe, let alone dignified.

Delightful Reflections

"Rudolph, the Virtual Reindeer" would clearly be a more relevant song to today's society.

It is morally wrong to stuff dynamite into unsuspecting people's stockings.

People who cheat on exams and/or their spouses deserve serious punishment!

Superstring bean entrees would probably be popular at theoretical physics conference dinners.

Parents who argue that TV programming should contain more violence to better prepare children to understand the real world in which they will be living may be misguided.

It would be grossly irresponsible to give a bullhorn as a holiday gift to someone who already has four convictions for disturbing the peace.

Stealing toilet paper from fast food restaurants is morally reprehensible!

It is at best questionably ethical to bribe Santa Claus to put one's siblings on the naughty list.

Putting up a big banner saying that "Thanksgiving sucks!" is a possible indication of lack of gratitude.

It is doubtful that more than 5% of the general population would have an interest in having more than four partridges on pear trees.

Someone who changes the "Hey Jude" lyrics to "Take a sad song and make it badder" might be vulnerable to criticism of both his or her grammar and level of pessimism.

Adulterous serial killers who sell critical military technology to the enemy and cheat on their taxes are disgusting psychopaths.

To the extent possible, homeowners have a moral obligation to resist temptation and turn burglars over to the police rather than feeding them to the sharks.

Children who hack into Santa's database to have themselves listed on the "nice" rather than "naughty" list are showing lack of gratitude and deserve to get coal for the rest of their lives!

The government of Nichtenstein may not be very accommodating.

The Green Tea Party might support alternative energy.

It would be rather demoralizing to receive an unsolicited letter from a bank stating that one has been pre-disapproved for a credit card.

It would be an act of tremendous honesty if manufacturers of low quality food products had a "worst if used after" date on their products.

Parents who have selected a first name for a son beginning with the letter "D" should not choose the middle name Merit.

A semi-psycho is still a relatively bad person.

Enlisting the aid of aliens from outer space to cheat on an exam is incredibly reprehensible!

Sending out fake Christmas cards is at best a questionable practice and quite possibly inappropriate.

Adultery, disturbing the peace, ditching classes with impunity, surfing the Internet during class, and complaining about grades are way uncool!

It does not make sense to promise a rose garden to someone who has repeatedly told you that he or she can't stand roses.

A song titled "Singing in Bahrain" might help promote tourism.

Bullying someone into signing a petition against bullying is rather hypocritical.

It is morally reprehensible to put fake periodic tables with incorrect information in classrooms.

People who ignore a T-shirt saying that "My big sister is going to beat the [expletive deleted] out of people who insult my grandmother" have at least been warned.

One would be justified in not being entirely confident in the contents of candy bars made at a chocolate factory called Willie Whacko.

It is mean to continuously text "Repent your sins!" to someone that you know has already repented.

Students who dis their professors have a seriously messed up value system!

It is likely that few letters to Santa Claus ask for paper towels.

A history doctoral dissertation whose main conclusion is that Karl Marx was a communist would probably not be much of a scholarly contribution.

There would probably be significant logistical problems in requiring the drunken sailor to attend in-person AA meetings as a condition for his continued employment.

Bragging that "My sister is 3.1% meaner than your sister" is really not all that impressive.

Those who give in to extortion attempts by trick-or-treaters should limit the spoils to very small pieces. Halloween is a great time to be stingy!

It is a plausible a claim that trick-or-treaters have become 23.5% greedier over the last five years.

It would be reasonable for a prosecutor to seek to have a prospective juror observed to be reading a book titled The Joy of Flaunting Antitrust Law With Impunity excused for cause—especially for a criminal trial alleging conspiracy to engage in anti-competitive behavior.

A bumper sticker saying that "My Dachshund is better than your Dachshund!" would arguably be deceptive if the owner of the car did not, in fact, have a Dachshund.

Despite the best intentions of a parent, giving a young person a book titled The Only Guide to Serial Mugging That You Will Ever Need would send the wrong message.

Children who stay home to reflect on their sins rather than going trick-or-treating will likely experience greater moral growth.

It should be cause for rather serious concern if one overhears a son or daughter saying that "It's so much easier to turn people over to organized crime figures than to try to talk sense into them."

> A bumper sticker saying that "My grandpa is a mean SOB" could be considered insulting to one's great-grandmother.

> Even in Southern California, it is more likely that there will be a white Christmas than that children will actually listen.

> Children would be better off—both intellectually and health wise—getting school supplies instead of candy on Halloween.

> The hypothesis that empathy can neither be created nor destroyed is intriguing, but it is doubtful that it would hold up.

> Most reasonable people would, on the balance, probably not support the repeal of laws against dueling.

Naming a daughter Disgrace is at best unkind.

A pessimist might admonish Jude to "Take a happy song and make it more realistic."

A minister who, after his Sunday sermon on the Ten Commandments, stole a car to get to his mistress (stopping on the way to participate in a pagan ritual), told his mother when she called to "Shut up for G***'s sake," told the police that his neighbor had stolen the car, killed a witness who could have testified otherwise, and coveted one of his parishioners' semi-automatic rifle would seem to be acting rather hypocritically.

When in Rome, it may be thankless task to point out to the Romans the error of their ways.

- Is there such a thing as a Jakarta envelope? If so, what would it look like?

- It is better to trick than to treat obnoxious children coming to extort candy on Halloween.

- A carol with the lyrics "We wish you a rated X-mas and a sleazy new year" would be quite unwholesome!

- It is unethical for bail bonds people to put up signs saying "Thank you for disturbing the peace!"

- Is there, in some parallel universe, a well known band named the Yellow Floyd and a major hit named "Pink Submarine?"

One should probably be suspicious of a student claiming to have missed an exam due to pre-remissive elephantoid cirrhosis of the medium sized intestine.

It is doubtful that a court headed by an Injustice of the Peace would provide sufficient substantive and procedural due process protection.

The phrase "The best part of waking up is Folger's in your cup" likely has vastly different meanings if uttered by an optimist and a pessimist.

Living in the yellow submarine would most likely be rather inconvenient—especially if no crane is available to help move furniture in and out.

A designer named Calvin Cain might make sinful and revealing clothing that would not facilitate harmony among siblings.

It is not a good idea to throw snowballs or water balloons at Santa Claus.

Off hand, it would be difficult to respond to the argument that begging someone's pardon is undignified.

Petty Theft—Toy Car would not be an appropriate video game for children, either.

It would seem somewhat disillusioning to find out, after all these years, that an ounce of prevention is actually only worth 15.35 oz. of cure.

A gift subscription to Redneck Living is probably not an effective way to ingratiate oneself with important decision makers.

Barack could have promised Michelle a rose garden back in December 2008 without having to worry much about delivering.

Smoking an exhaust pipe is even dumber than smoking tobacco.

One should probably hesitate to hire an applicant with numerous convictions for disturbing the peace for the position of Head Librarian.

It is doubtfully that most people would be successful in trying to disprove the Pythagorean Theorem.

Hiring an applicant for a physicist position might not be appropriate if he or she has taken most of his or her coursework in a Department of Science Fiction.

Grandparents who write profanity laden birthday cards are setting a very bad example.

Members of the Ice Tea Party might be a bit on the cold side.

Sadly, one rarely ever hears children bragging to their friends that "My character is more morally wholesome than your character!"

One would be justified in questioning the mental stability of an individual who walks up to randomly selected strangers and announces that "I kill for Santa Claus!"

If morning has broken, it has hopefully not been damaged beyond repair.

It would be ironic if Warren Buffett prefers to order a la carte.

Students who complain about not being given a sufficient workload should be grateful for what they actually got.

As an astronomical reference point, the Puny Dipper would probably be unimpressive and easy to miss.

It is unconscionable to dress up in a Santa Claus suit and drop off packages of one's garbage in the guise of presents

> If the Beatles had been active today instead of so much earlier, they might have recorded "Blackberry Features Forever."

> If Jenny gives her mother a T-shirt saying that "My daughter is better than your daughter," some people might get the impression that Jenny's mother—rather than Jenny—is rather immodest.

> One would have to agree with the former Cat Stevens that it is unrealistic to expect jeans to last forever—even if a patch is applied.

> A voice mail greeting to customers that "Your call is relatively important to us" would probably come across as relatively honest but somewhat under-enthusiastic.

In the interest of efficiency, many people today will probably text the barber on Penny Lane rather than taking the time to stop by to say hello.

Profanity should generally be avoided during a job interview.

It would be a bit of a disgrace for a male elephant to forget his wife's birthday.

One ought not hang out in psycho-space.

Students on roller skates, although inconvenient, are much preferable to cheapskates who will be stingy in their alumni contributions to the University.

One should not count on an appeals court to overturn a conviction based on the 57th Amendment.

There might be money to be made on an instant disciplinary messaging service that would do the dirty work for parents who want to avoid having to chew out misbehaving children themselves.

Columbus would have been a bit of a sophist if he had insisted that flat screen TVs are actually round.

It is highly inappropriate for jurors to go through several beers while listening to an afternoon of testimony.

It is truly reprehensible to climb up a pineapple tree and throw a big one down on someone sleeping below.

Pledging Pi Iota Gamma (PIG) is really not advisable.

Was LeRoy Brown just a few percentage points worse than old King Kong or greatly more so?

Those who select the DISH network to get extra juicy coverage might be disappointed.

A T-shirt or bumper sticker saying "Morally Repugnant is Cool!" is morally repugnant (and way uncool!)

Children—however sincere and well intentioned they may be—should not include a recommendation in their letters to Santa that he go on a diet.

- It is ironic that the right to use bullet points may be protected by both the First and Second Amendments.

- Did Crystal Gayle ever find out why her ex-significant other had left the one he had left her for?

- It is almost certainly true that most pigs can, in fact, not fly, but we cannot definitively rule out the possibility of a giant cover-up by farmers worried about liability.

- It is not clear in which ways cultured pearls differ from redneck ones.

- Avoiding Route 66 may or may not be an effective way to avoid getting kicked.

It is morally wrong to put fake parking tickets on disliked others' windshields—especially if the car is actually parked legally.

It is clearly morally wrong to replace hotel Bibles with fake ones saying that adultery is OK.

It is generally not a good idea to squirt water guns—especially super-soakers—at highway patrol officers.

Returning a letter for a previous resident at one's address to the sender with a notation that "This disgusting psychopath is no longer at this address" might result in a libel suit and/or hurt feelings.

Kidney piercing is incredibly stupid.

It is not clear how many adulterers it takes to change a light bulb, but one should definitely not take the word of a group of them that they did so at face value.

Obnoxious children might like to sing "Noisy Night" during the holidays.

It is not easy to find the zip code for the Gettysburg Address.

It would likely violate social norms to forcefully shove someone out of the way and exclaim "¡Sin permiso!"

It would seem rather hostile to exclaim "Curse you!" when someone sneezes.

A remote controlled bird in the bush is not necessarily worth a lot less than one in the hand.

It is not advisable to name a jewelry store Pathetic Pearls.

Candidates for public office would be well advised to pass on the slogan "Slash people, not budgets."

Decent society would really have no choice but to strongly disapprove of an organization called Fathers Against Sober Driving (FASD).

Prudent parents ought to skeptical of an "all natural" herbal supplement whose manufacturer claims that it protects children from the dangers of the Internet.

Scummy scumbags are scummy!

Most people are probably not quite positive that they know what Neil Diamond means.

It is probably not a good idea to use the domain name ThisDump.com for a hotel web site.

It is probably not safe—no matter how well intentioned—to tell a bank robber that he or she really should go home and pray to be sure that this is the right thing to do before proceeding.

If handed a business card by someone with the title of "Facilitator of Fraud," one really has an obligation to pass it on to the FBI and/or local law enforcement.

It is doubtful that anyone wearing a CIA wind breaker is actually with the Agency.

It is not clear what one should make of a proverb that "Pigs don't grow on trees."

Members of Bimbos Without Borders might be rather unselective in the people they party with.

A child wearing a T-shirt saying "The [expletive deleted] youth pastor told my [expletive deleted] grandma to [expletive deleted] shut her [expletive deleted] mouth. [Expletive deleted] cool!" is likely to exacerbate the conflict.

Messing with the Mossad is rather stupid.

- Locating a luxury resort at Basura Bay is likely a rather poor idea.

- A supposedly fancy restaurant named Chez le Cochon should probably give cause for hesitation.

- A subscription to Trash for Tough Teens is a very inappropriate birthday gift.

- An exasperated crime family patriarch might tell a grandchild that "You're no bad!"

- A sign proclaiming "Free Delivery" would have a different meaning at a restaurant and a hospital.

Non-confidential informants probably have a relatively short remaining life expectancy.

Senior citizens who—without any provocation—beat up motorcycle riders are engaging in an unconscionable act of bullying.

It is not clear if a Hazelnutcase is more serious than a walnutcase.

One ought to be apprehensive about an individual Googling the phrase "recipes for disaster."

Critical viewers might have serious concerns about a cartoon series called The Pink Panda. What would happen to the spots?

The Second Amendment may not protect the right to bear nuclear arms.

Most school principals would probably not be appreciative of students taking up a collection to cover the costs of shipping an unpopular teacher to Australia.

A movie titled Sinful in Seattle would likely feature a rather unwholesome plot.

Photoshop really ought to stay open 24/7.

Most Americans would unquestionably resent receiving a tax bill from some foreign country's External Revenue Service.

Prince Charles may not like the idea of royalty-free music.

Murder is mean.

Paucity of profit is positively pathetic.

A City of Zero Sinners would seem a bit elitist and self righteous.

Chewing tobacco is highly inappropriate during a State dinner at the White House.

An individual wearing an "I ♥ heart surgery" button is more likely to be a cardiac surgeon than a patient.

The reassurance that "You're not a serious psycho" is really not a genuine compliment.

Recommending an Execution MBA program to disliked co-workers might have a rather chilling effect.

One would have reason to be suspicious of a job applicant claiming to have a degree in computer science from the Massachusetts Institute of Theology.

As a matter of pragmatics, being able to tell whether or not it is a duck may not be particularly essential unless you are a farmer, hunter, or chef.

It is generally not worthwhile and appropriate to file Federal habeas appeals over parking tickets.

A rather far fetched hypothesis of the origin of the wording of the First Amendment is that someone offhandedly remarked, "You know, Congress really should make no law respecting an establishment of religion, or prohibiting the free exercise thereof; or abridging the freedom of speech, or of the press; or the right of the people peaceably to assemble, and to petition the Government for a redress of grievances. Such laws would be way uncool!"

Hopefully, good children are not having nightmares that Santa Claus will be called to serve on a sequestered jury lasting through the holidays.

Moral Fiber Deficiency Syndrome (MFDS) is not a legitimate excuse for adultery, securities fraud, spitting on librarians, disturbing the peace, armed robbery, plagiarism, theft of electricity, assault with a deadly (or non-deadly) weapon, counterfeiting, and reading filthy magazines.

A psychopath who takes out a Yellow Page ad under the category of "Traitors" would run a fairly significant risk of getting caught.

Many people would probably have liked math better if there had been a greater emphasis on deferential equations.

I am not entirely convinced that the problem is all inside Paul Simon's mind.

A letter ostensibly from a psychiatrist asking for accommodations for a student due to Egodystonic Self Aggranditization Syndrome (ESAS) ought to raise suspicions.

One might suspect that a button worn by a criminal defendant saying "Sanity is for suckers!" is a ploy rather than a genuine indication of mental incapacity.

One rarely ever hears the term "sitting goose."

If a friend lends you a vacation home, it is mean to rekey the locks.

Forging prescriptions for OTC products is stupid.

The artist likely had a strange sense of humor—and quite possibly a penchant for rebelling against reality—if the painting "Probably a Pig" featured a Dachshund and "Definitely a Dachshund" featured a pig.

One should be cautious of a no strings detached deal.

Lives of parents whose children suffer from Attention Surplus-Hypoactivity Disorder (ASHD) are likely to be a lot easier.

It is amazing how long pie with ice cream has managed to stayed in fashion.

It is not advisable for academics to wear a T-shirt with the word "Reviewer" and a bull's eye target at conferences.

There may not be whole lot of reason to care about indifferential equations.

Theoretical physicists would likely be disappointed if they found the Higgs Bozo instead of the Boson.

Most likely, fewer than 45% of Americans over the age of 50 believe in Santa Claus.

One should not count on an oversized pancake breakfast at the Healthnut Hotel.

Few people seem to be questioning the authenticity of Bruce Springsteen's birth certificate.

It is cruel to sing "Santa Claus ain't comin' to town" to children who have not misbehaved.

Conspiracy to carol—especially during the holiday season—should be probably not be a cause for great concern.

Someone who says "Ask not what your country can do for you; ask what you and your country can do for me" is probably rather selfish.

It would be ironic if there is no jail in Casa Grande, AZ.

It is unclear if a T-shirt saying "Not Wanted by FBI!" is expressing relief or bemoaning rejection.

Profit is paramount!

A certificate of inauthenticity would probably not add that much value to a painting.

A red neck tie is likely to be more elegant than a redneck tie.

A T-shirt saying "My brother belongs in the doghouse!" might be motivated by sibling rivalry (or the lack of it if the wearer is a dog).

Few confirmed cases of Vitamin B39 deficiency have been reported recently.

Hopefully, Jackson Browne has had a chance to refuel.

> If only more students would believe in the doctrine of professorial infallibility!

> Someone who signs a letter to an advice columnist "Measly in Michigan" might have a self esteem problem.

> Telling a child that "My grandmother is going to punish your grandmother for your sins" is not a good lesson in justice.

> Decent society ought to disapprove of mediocre and morally marginal material.

> At some point, Willie Nelson will probably want to get off the road again.

It is doubtful that medical marijuana is a safe and effective treatment for Moral Fiber Deficiency Syndrome. It is morally wrong for physicians to prescribe it for this purpose.

Cat and zebra shows seem to be rather rare events.

An audience would probably not like to hear a speaker say, "To make a long story longer and more boring...."

Having a black tie event at the Rowdy Redneck Restaurant might be considered a form of reverse snobbery.

Not many people or organizations appear to be hosting their websites at StopMommy.com.

- Hopefully, Self Actualization Through Disturbing the Peace will not become a bestseller.

- It is probably quite an honor to be introduced by an organized crime figure as "my bad friend...."

- Singing "We Ain't the Champions" could be a possible collective sign of modesty or low self-esteem.

- Profit is more satisfying than parties.

- It may not be effective for fight promoters to think outside the box.

- A serial killer targeting doughnut shop employees would likely be a very high priority for police.

"Good children don't grow on trees, either!" is a rather cynical comeback.

Wearing a T-shirt saying that "My handler is better than your handler!" is likely a breach of security.

Someone who calls a physician asking him or her to make a house call to an apple plantation might be dismissed as a crank.

It is probably not worth the effort to try to borrow a cup of sugar from a neighbor whose mailbox bears the name Mean Molly.

It is unlikely that many whales spend a lot of time trying to save the people.

Police officers who believe that an apple fritter a day will keep the doctor away are probably succumbing to wishful thinking.

It is unlikely that the CIA recruits through classified advertisements.

It is stupid to ask for Google Minus when you can get Google Plus.

It doesn't seem fair to tell someone who takes offense at a poem with the words "Pigs are pathetic/ And so are you" that he or she is just "overly sensitive."

A movie or TV series called The Three Racketeers would set a very bad example for children.

It is unlikely that more than 30% of women would appreciate a gift from in-laws of a T-shirt with the message "I ♥ obeying my husband! He knows what's best for me." Most of those who would appreciate such a gift are probably over the age of 35.

Someone who goes with the slogan "Sell the whales!" is likely greedy or at least has an entrepreneurial bent.

There is some ambiguity in the assertion that "My great grandmother hauled your pathetic grandmother off to the slammer."

Children and teenagers who encourage their friends to obey their parents are helping make this a better world.

Committing parole violations in a doughnut shop is rather stupid.

When trying to evade an enemy, it is better to LOS than to LOL.

Women are more likely to persuade husbands or boyfriends to go along on a "strategic supply mission" than a "shopping trip."

It is probably not a good idea to walk up and seek clarification from someone wearing a T-shirt saying "I am your second worst nightmare."

A hack license is not a legitimate excuse for taxi drivers who attempt to break into computer networks.

Delightful Reflections

www.ingramcontent.com/pod-product-compliance
Lightning Source LLC
Chambersburg PA
CBHW071514040426
42444CB00008B/1644